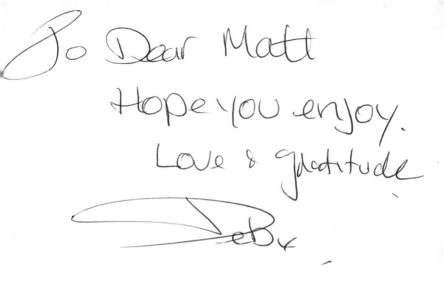

To Dear Matt
Hope you enjoy.
Love & gratitude

Deb x

A Spiritual Budget

Seven Steps to Financial Freedom

Debbie Seaton

BALBOA
PRESS
A DIVISION OF HAY HOUSE

Balboa Press books may be ordered through booksellers or by contacting:

Balboa Press
A Division of Hay House
1663 Liberty Drive
Bloomington, IN 47403
www.balboapress.com.au
1-(877) 407-4847

ISBN: 978-1-4525-0941-9 (sc)
ISBN: 978-1-4525-0944-0 (e)

Printed in the United States of America

Balboa Press rev. date: 05/07/2013

"You can never know what you think; you can only ever know what you feel. That is why the great teachers have always said that feelings are the eyes of the heart. Thinking about feeling is not the same as feeling. Thinking about reality is not the same as experiencing reality. For you as a soul journeying through eternity, your feelings are the synthesis of everything you experience— your sensations, emotions, thoughts and ideas. Embracing this synthesis without judgment is the key to understanding, revelation, inner peace and lasting personal spiritual growth"

Michael King
http://michaelking.id.au

A *Spiritual Budget* is dedicated to

Michael and Segolene King, Linda Koen and the unseen. Without their inspiration, this book would not have eventuated. Everything I have learnt over the last 11 years has been through the teachings of the Cosmosis Mentoring Centre and for this I am eternally grateful.

www.mysteryschool.org.au

And to my brother, John Seaton

And to my children—Lisa, David and Janelle and my beautiful grandchildren Gabrielle, Sam, Emmett, Daemon, Hayden and little Frankie, who are always close to my heart.

Contents

Foreword

It is with enormous pleasure and gratitude I feel right now, that I begin to write the foreword to Debbie Seaton's "A *Spiritual Budget—The Seven Steps to Financial Freedom.*" If you feel so inspired and allow these magical steps to unfold, the very pages that follow from here will begin the most incredible journey of healing and transformation, like none you may ever have experienced before. When you read this book, you may feel just like you have Debbie sitting right there with you on the couch, gently encouraging you over a cup of tea, loving and supporting you like no one has done so before and really hearing you—that very part of you that longs to be heard and acknowledged. You quite possibly may start to feel a growing sense of direction and a heightened state of possibility that just may increase after each chapter. I now know what that is called—it is HOPE!

Like many of you reading this foreword, you may understand how it feels to have those mountains of bills that keep piling up secretly at the back of the filing cabinet! Those bills that may not even have been opened to see the light of day yet, from the fear of knowing what's in them.

You may know the kind of 'lack' that has nothing to do with money. To feel poor in the kind of love that you really deserve, that everyone deserves in life!

Accompanying all states of 'lack', are the mountains of pain and fear that fill you up so deep within, you forget what it's like to be without that low-grade anxiousness running in the background of your life. It's strange how we never really think anyone else can see it (though you spend so much of your precious time and energy trying to conceal and avoid feeling it!)

I, too, knew how it felt to be full of disappointment in life and of life's lost opportunities, no matter how subtle or strong it may be playing out in the day to day-ness.

So, picture this. One day Debbie Seaton walked into my house. We had just begun entertaining the possibility of working together to help me move forward in my life, financially and otherwise. On that day, I was possibly at my lowest ebb. Quite literally, I was on the floor, facing some harsh realities of where I was at in life. I felt utterly hopeless and was seriously going around in circles.

To give you the complete visual—I was broke. I was without a job. I felt like I was unemployable and finished. I was severely depressed and entertaining suicidal thoughts. I was grossly overweight and felt very ashamed and unattractive. I was in debt and my bank was talking 'foreclosure' on my unit. I was single and alone and on a government pension. Worst of all, I was feeling very sorry for myself and was pushing away everyone around me as a result.

This compounded my feelings of isolation and I felt the world and everyone in it secretly hated me. I was judging and hating so much of myself and projecting all of this out into the world. I really felt like I couldn't be helped. I was my own worst enemy and I felt lost. It's no wonder my life was in pieces, when you see what I was focusing on.

Many wonderful mentors and healers had assisted me in the past and yet here I was, still yo-yoing around through life, one step forward, and several steps back. I was still annoyingly not actualizing what I had surely come to do to make a difference in this life and frustration was at the core of my despair.

What Debbie did initially for me was to show me how to empower myself to heal and grow and how to accept myself. Firstly, I had to stop doing that which was causing me harm. I learnt that what happens in your life, on the outside, is quite often a perfect mirror reflection for what's going down on the 'inside'.

I learnt that until I fully got on board with myself, learnt to love, respect and accept myself, (especially at my worst), then even if God himself had popped in and created a miracle and said "Jacqui, you are healed!", sadly I wouldn't have believed it and it would have been a waste!

I learnt that until you heal that which is within, all the baggage, the default shonky programs, the taught behaviours and responses that are so often shaped and learnt when we are so young, we are just like a computer with a bunch of nasty viruses on board and some very out-dated software, running on auto command!

Debbie's *Seven Steps to Financial Freedom* actually unfolded in perfect timing. For me, it was a simple choice of doing what she said and trusting her. I had no other place to go than up.

Then Debbie opened me up to the true spirit of gratitude.

One of the other most incredible keys to transforming loss and lack in life is embracing the gift of gratitude. Debbie quite literally embodies gratitude. I know we've often heard that 'love makes the world go around' and really that's true. However, until I could feel love, gratitude was the first step, which then ignited the love within me. Funny how when I look back, I used to actually hate gratitude, as it challenged my investment I had in feeling sorry for myself. Initially, I found it very challenging to identify anything for which to be grateful. So, using some of Debbie's steps and tools, we worked on this until I was able to really *feel* it. And bit by bit, 'faking it till I made it' sometimes, I actually did start to *feel* it. This was the single, most profound thing I believe I have learnt. Through gratitude, truly all things are possible. You can let go of that which no longer serves you and install some wondrous new ways of being and doing.

What also came about from gratitude was a deeper love and respect for myself. You can't judge yourself or your actions when you are holding gratitude for you and your life. Yes, ALL of it! I know that possibly sounds a bit corny, but I realized that in holding more respect and gratitude for myself, I started to see that some of the so-called 'disasters' in my life, have actually become some of my greatest gifts. It's as a result of my life, that I can come to this place of healing and change, uniquely, that would not have happened otherwise. Gratitude is a choice and I choose it daily.

The momentum picked up as Debbie's program unfolded and I was able to hold steady and in each step, my life quite literally started taking shape—patience and baby steps to begin with. A growing sense of accomplishment and joy has grounded in my life and I now feel capable of stretching myself in places I could only have dreamt of before. Another of the golden keys for me was 'not giving up'. This is without doubt one of Debbie's strongest points. She never gives up on life or on herself or on anyone with whom she works. Having her as my mentor and following her program for the 12 months I was with her, certainly gave me a first-hand experience of what is required to just keep going. Some of us never had such role models in our lives and so it has been a special gift that Debbie has bestowed upon me—the true influence of the abundance of love, abundance of caring, abundance of hope and above all a huge abundance of joy.

I could so easily write more. However, I invite you now to sit back, get relaxed, make yourself a cup of tea and start at Chapter One. If you simply allow the process to unfold and allow transformation, hope and joy to ground and shine forth in your life, this will be the journey of your life.

Enjoy the journey. It's your choice right here, right now!

Jacqui Sheales, Life Coach & Mentor
www.wholenesshealing.com.au

Introduction

It has been quite a journey these last years—how I became a Life Coach and Mentor and a Financial Counsellor and how I integrated this new learning into 11 years of my own journey of self-discovery. There is a saying "when the student is ready, the teacher will come". I have been blessed to find a most wonderful mentor, Michael King, who has walked beside me so supportively, lovingly and patiently. He has taught me how to feel again and empowered me to be myself, to be authentic and to be the best I can be. He has taught me how to leave the old behind and to keep walking forever forward.

Born in Sydney, Australia, the eldest of four children, my childhood was tough and financial hardship was 'the norm'. Both my parents were in the grip of severe addictions. Life was an emotional roller coaster and a journey of rejection and abandonment. It was a struggle to survive.

When I was eight my parents separated (my mother left to find happiness with another man). Our father was incapable of caring for us. My five-year-old brother and I were not wanted and it was soul-destroying to be unwanted at such a young age. Eventually, we went to live with our grandfather and his wife, which was sadly a totally loveless environment.

Every day my brother and I would find a safe place to hide where we would sit and hold hands and share stories with each other and dream of how our mum was coming back to get us, to take us away and to love us again.

We eventually went back to live with our mother after four years. There were many memories over the years—in particular, the birth and death of a baby sister who touched my heart for three weeks before she sadly left us. Then there was my mother and stepfather's emotional and physical abuse and alcohol addiction. There are many sad and painful accounts from my childhood. That is where I came from, yet this is not who I am now.

Meeting my husband when I was 17 years old (the marriage lasted 34 years) happily helped me escape from a tormented life. It was a joy and I was so grateful to him for a life so far removed from my experiences in childhood. Our eldest daughter was born six weeks before we were married, a few days before my twentieth birthday. Over the next four years, a son and a younger daughter came into our lives. We lived in Sydney for the first 18 months of our marriage and then moved to Bathurst, a large country town in NSW. My fondest memories are that of my children. I smile inside and out at their wonderful sense of humour and their ability to see the funny side of life. Of course, along the years there were trials and tribulations as children grow and experience their teenage years. I feel so blessed to be their mum, seeing them now married with children of their own.

Sadly, the marriage was starting to break down. I had taken the path of self-discovery and my husband had not. As I was growing and expanding more, so very determined to explore who I really was, a gap had started to appear between us and we inevitably grew too far apart. There were times when we nearly left each other and we would relent and give the marriage another chance, but this would only smooth things over for a short time. Finally, it was time. We had given it our best and we both decided to move on. We divorced, as friends, and both embarked on our separate journeys.

I found myself alone at 52, starting a new life on the other side of Australia in Perth. Being so far away from my children and grandchildren was challenging. Even though I have many friends, the feeling of living and being totally alone without the responsibility of another was strange. This was an opportunity to explore and to delve deeper into myself. It was quite an experience, as I faced the tidal wave of emotions of what I had avoided and denied throughout my life. It felt so deep, like many lifetimes joined into one. Even though there was support around me, nothing or no-one could fill the emptiness I felt inside.

In truth, it was time to face the fear and the illusion of the 'I can't' beliefs taken on from what I had been told and what I had created for myself. I realised that I had learnt to endure life, to take the good times with the bad while constantly compromising and invalidating myself. My self-esteem was low and I was crippled by the fear of rejection. My life was always about others. I had no idea what I wanted or needed.

My first food-shopping experience on my own was one of walking around a supermarket on the brink of tears because for the life of me I could not pinpoint what *I* liked to eat. I found myself walking to the checkout with just the bare essentials in the bottom of the trolley. There was also the question of how I was going to make a living. I had injured myself at work 12 years previously and had endured two major surgeries. On top of that my employers retired me on a disability pension from my superfund and told me I would never be able to work again.

My situation was grim and confronting. There was my age and my disability and I found myself being caught up in the boxes, limitations, labels and systems that society imposed on me in order to control how I should look or what I should believe in. And I bought into those limitations. I take responsibility for that.

But one day, mustering the courage, I walked into an employment agency. A girl about 18 years old promptly told me that I needed to be re-trained, but that the likelihood of finding a job at my age with a disability from an injury would go against me in the workforce. I was referred to a government body and was assigned a case worker who re-trained people like me—those in the 'too old with a disability' box. I was sent to doctors and assessed and told that if I ever did find a job, I would only be able to work a limited number of hours a week.

Debbie Seaton

Determined to find a career a few years earlier, I had completed a *Certificate IV in Community Services*, which helped my predicament—at least it was a direction. I had also begun a course in *Mentoring and Life Coaching*, which was also helpful. But how was I going to use these skills? What job could I get with no experience? I pondered this for a very long time. Then the answer came—I would be a Financial Counsellor! My heart started to sing. I could work with people like me and be able to give back from my own life experience!

With hope in my heart, I enrolled myself in a *Diploma of Community Services* specialising in Financial Counselling. It was an 18 month course and I found myself very busy with two courses to complete. I was feeling the challenge I had given myself. It was a difficult time, always having doubts about my abilities and constantly judging myself. It was a long process, which pushed me beyond the limitations I had imposed upon myself.

Regularly visiting my case worker (who was supposed to be assisting me to get back into the workforce) was depressing, to say the least. It didn't matter how positive my attitude was, it felt like I was being held back and I was given absolutely no encouragement or belief in my ability to succeed.

Then it hit me hard—why everything felt like such a challenge. I realised that I had to break free from the system, from the "I can't, I am too old", disability box in which I had allowed myself to be caught up. My hope and self-determination started to grow again, really affirming that I could succeed.

For part of my training as a Financial Counsellor, I was placed two days a week volunteering with a Financial Counselling service. This was a blessing and provided the much-needed skills and experience to apply for a Financial Counselling position.

Finally finishing my *Certificate IV in Mentoring and Life Coaching* course gave me some confidence to start lifting the lid on the box, the system, out of which I was determined to break. I became grateful to the case worker who was assigned to me. Her lack of encouragement and her 'ability' to always find obstacles and hurdles had only made my self-determination stronger. I continued my studies with only six months to go and it felt like it was time to take that step up—and find a job.

While attending our monthly Financial Counselling workshop, I overheard news of a possible job. It was full-time and without hesitation I decided right then and there to apply. The next day I sent my resume in and to my surprise (within hours) they contacted me to come in for an interview! I couldn't believe it. I was offered the job and told I could start the very next day!

However, there was one glitch. The position was only for three months and I wasn't allowed to work on top of the pension I already received. So, I had to make the decision to let the past go, let my pension go and trust that I would be OK. I rang the case worker and told her of my decision. There was nothing she could say. It was done! I had broken the system, moved back into living and trusted myself.

I have had a full life of experience and have learnt to keep walking forward and to never look back with regret. I do not stop for anyone or anything for I create my own reality and my future. What really amuses me is that the profession I chose as a Financial Counsellor is what I call 'system busting', meaning that I can make a difference. I have learnt to transform my own self-imposed limitations and those that society and the system put in place to keep me small and controlled. I am so enjoying life on my journey along the path of self-discovery, ever learning new things. I am unstoppable in stepping into to my plan and purpose, exploring within my own self why I am here on this beautiful planet.

Looking back at my parents, how I grew up and the journey that has brought me to this very moment, I now have so much more understanding of how everyone in my life has done their best through their own life experience. I have learnt that within life there is always a choice. I can either stay in my comfort zone (never taking a risk and slowly dying inside), or I can step out of the box to live a rich life that goes way beyond anything my parents could have dreamed.

Like many, they gave in to what they believed about themselves, never allowing themselves to wonder if they could have been so much more. They didn't realise that they could have reached for the stars and beyond, if only they hadn't identified with the boxes, limitations and judgments they allowed and believed in, which was learned from their parents, teaches, peers, religion and society. *Thanks mum and dad for being the best you could be and showing me how to be more. I understand now that you did the best you could through your own life experiences. I thank you both for bringing me into this world to learn to love and grow and to experience a full life.*

There is nothing wrong with making mistakes. Learning from them is perfection.

What I have learnt in life is to acknowledge how I have lived, how I have felt and what I have learnt, to be grateful for all my experiences, whatever they have been, to never judge them (as we can always make a new choice) and to let the old choices of our past go. This is how we bring harmony in our lives.

Chapter 1

Abundance and Gratitude

Living to the beat of your drum

"It's not what's happening to you now or what has happened in the past that determines who you become. Rather, it's your decisions about what to focus on, what things mean to you and what you are going to do about them that will determine your ultimate destiny."

Tony Robbins

The key to abundance, success and embracing our potential is **Gratitude** and being loving and accepting of our self throughout our life experience.

Abundance is achieved when we are the captain of our ship and become in charge and responsible for all aspects of our lives. How we think and express ourselves by our speech and body language in a loving positive way can bring joy into our lives and inspire all around us.

Are you grateful and do you appreciate what you have in your life? Are you focusing on abundance or lack? Whether it is a relationship in turmoil, financial pressure, poor health or problems in a job, negative situations arise because of a lack of gratitude over a long period of time. If we are not grateful for each and everything in our lives, we are unintentionally taking those things for granted.

When we don't give thanks in return we stop the magic happening in our lives.

Do you hold the belief that the Universe is infinitely abundant? If you focus on lack, she will honour your choices and you will receive lack. If you are grateful and focus on the wonder and on all you have in life, the Universe will honour your choices and abundance will continue to flow in all areas of your life.

Let's look at changing our attitudes and looking to see how we can change the 'beat of our drum'. Are you constantly beating to the rhythm of "I can't, I can't afford it, nobody likes me, I don't fit in, I haven't got enough time, I can't get a job, I don't have any money"? What do you think about yourself? Are your thoughts empowering you or do you put yourself down? Addressing our attitude, by working with gratitude, observing behaviour and reprogramming our thoughts takes effort and practice and the rewards are immense.

Start building your 'gratitude muscle' by buying yourself a beautiful journal in your favourite colour so you can write down everything in your life for which you are grateful. When we are grateful it changes our lives. We become more aware and begin to appreciate all the wonderful blessings we have already received.

Here are some tips to kick-start you on the road to building your gratitude muscle:

- Look around and take notice of what you take for granted.
- Look at the big, the small and the in between things that are in your everyday life.
- What about you specifically, are you grateful for?
- What are your favourite foods?

- What music do you like?
- Do you have a special friend you enjoy spending time with, are you grateful for having this friend in your life?
- Do you have a family, a partner or children? What joy do they bring into your life for which you are grateful?
- How about walking, exercising and being with nature?

Saying affirmations will change the way we think and uplift our spirits.

Here are a few affirmations. Why not make up your own? It's fun!

- I am grateful for the flow of abundance in my life.
- I love to walk in nature's surroundings. I am grateful for the flowers and trees and the beauty all around me.

- I am grateful for what I have achieved and myself.
- I am grateful for not worrying what people think and I am finding more of who I am every day.
- I am grateful for all experiences in my life.

Gratitude is something we can work on every day for the rest of our lives. Let's explore our attitudes and how our thoughts create our reality. If we choose to see ourselves as a victim of life and our thoughts are negative, we have an attitude of 'poor me' and we live life as a drama, instead of embracing the lessons and gifts that life and the universe have to offer.

As we choose to live a life full of positive thoughts and have an optimistic view, we see life as less of a struggle. We look for solutions and do our best in each and every moment and we beat our drum to 'I am, I can, I will' and we see that success comes to us.

If we never look back over our shoulder and keep taking steps forward—even little steps—we will be rewarded and we will make wonderful progress. Show gratitude for every experience and have the courage to face and embrace every challenge with up cast eyes, always beating your drum to 'I am, I can, I will'. You will be amazed at how much success will come into your life. As we proceed along our path, it's important to remember that we must never judge ourselves. It doesn't matter if we make mistakes because we learn from them. Perfection is learning from your mistakes.

We all need tools to work with and one of my favourites is to do a nightly review of the day just gone—this is how awareness grows. So, every night I go through my day and I write it all down in a journal so it's all there in black and white and I can see where I can improve and how I can be my best. We can actually re-write our day to how we could have done things differently. By doing this, the next time we are faced with similar experiences, we are more likely to make different choices.

The Power of Choice

When life is difficult it is easy to get caught up in a feeling of fear. The way to deal with this is quite simple. We have two choices in life—either we choose love or we choose fear. The way to deal with this is quite simple. When we choose fear we blame others and become a victim to life and everything becomes about self. When we choose love we are able to see everything that happens as a gift. The universe is a wonderful mirror and everything reflects areas within our self that need growth and nurturing. Imagine an open doorway and on the other side of that door is what you have dreamed of. Your heart is open and you're singing with joy. You walk excitedly towards the door, but you find something is holding you back, blocking you from walking through, no matter how hard you push. You look down and notice you are carrying two large suitcases. What is in these suitcases? What are you holding onto? What are you not willing to let go of? What is stopping you from taking a step forward into your potential?

Gratitude is the key to moving past the baggage that we carry. When we have the courage to open the suitcase and face what we have stored away, then we can walk through the open door into our potential. We learn the truth is inside us and we don't have to look away for approval or to be validated. We accept ourselves for who we are. It is a true blessing to be able to look back and acknowledge how far we have come.

In each and every moment we have the Power of Choice. Here is an old Cherokee Legend that truly highlights the difference we can make in our life by the power of choice. Do we choose love or do we choose fear? What are you choosing?

A grandfather tells 'The Wolves Story' to his grandson

An old grandfather said to his grandson, who came to him with anger at a friend who did him an injustice, "Let me tell you a story."

"I, too, at times have felt great hate for those who have taken so much, with no sorrow for what they do.

But hate wears you down and does not hurt your enemy. It is like taking poison and wishing your enemy would die. I have struggled with these feelings many times."

He continued, "It is as if there are two wolves inside me

One is good and does no harm. He lives in harmony and all around him, and does not take offense, when no offense was intended. He will only fight when it is right to do so, and in the right way.

But the other wolf, ah! He is full of anger. The littlest thing will set him into a fit of temper. He fights everyone, all of the time, for no reason. He cannot think because of his anger, for his anger and hate are so great. It is helpless anger, for his anger will change nothing.

Sometimes, It is hard to live with these two wolves inside of me, for both of them try to dominate my spirit."

The boy looked intently into his grandfather's eyes and asked, "Which one wins, Grandfather?"

The Grandfather smiled and quietly said, "The one I feed"

So we see life is a choice and it's very empowering once we realise this. Do we choose to love, to inspire or do we choose to be negative and make life difficult for ourselves and all those around us? It is all our choice.

Chapter 2

How Are We at Paying Our Bills?

"Never spend your money before you have it"

Thomas Jefferson

"If we had no winter, the spring would not be so pleasant. If we did not sometimes experience adversity, prosperity would not be so welcome"

British Poet 1612-1672

Step 1 of A Spiritual Budget is Taking Responsibility

Putting away a small amount of money each week makes managing our lives so much easier. Learning how to budget and how not to spend more than we have are the key ingredients to being in control of your money. There are times in our lives when we experience difficulty and making ends meet seems impossible. This naturally affects us in all areas of our lives. In these times we feel anxiety and hopelessness for it doesn't matter how hard we try, nothing seems to go our way. We feel there is no one who will listen to us and we feel so very alone.

Some of us are embarrassed because of our financial situation and we can tend to feel a sense of failure. So we keep battling on, endeavouring to get ourselves out of the financial chaos when, in reality, we are only digging a deeper hole for ourselves. It is during these times that we must put our hand up and ask for help. It is a place where we face the truth and accept our circumstances. It takes courage to ask for help—to be so exposed when we are at our most vulnerable.

What is it we worry about most? Is it what our friends, family and society think of us? Do we allow ourselves to be weighed down by the pressures and stresses of life? The answer can be as easy as seeking the help of a financial counsellor in your area, preparing an income and expenditure sheet to determine exactly where you need assistance and learning about the options you have to overcome your difficulties.

When we do have the money to pay our bills, do we begrudge handing over our hard-earned money? If you have this attitude, you are not in the flow of abundance. Such an attitude represents scarcity and lack. Change your attitude and be grateful for utility bills that keep you warm in the winter and cool in the summer. They enable you to cook meals and listen to beautiful music and watch your favourite shows. Our utilities are services that make our lives so much easier.

Gratitude is the key that opens the door to success. Have a look around and see how much you do have for which to be grateful. It may be the relationships in your life, your garden or your family. It could be a job or just being able to put food on the table, or a warm bed to sleep in at night. One of the biggest challenges is to be grateful during those times when things are not going our way. It can be a challenge to appreciate and be grateful for what we deem to be the hard times in our lives.

At various stages in our lives we all experience difficult times. We lose our jobs, interest rates rise, we are faced with sickness and there are deaths in the family, accidents, separation and divorce. All these incidents have a major financial impact on our lives. It comes as a shock where one day we are comfortable and life is easy and within a matter of days we can be experiencing difficulty with little or no idea what to do or where to turn to next. Some choose to bury their heads in the sand in the hope that it will all go away. Denial is not the answer. What will work is learning to understand that during these times we need to rebuild our lives, sometimes starting from scratch. You will be surprised to find that in many instances we can emerge more the wiser from the experience.

We can become victims to the circumstances in our lives and live in "poor me" mode. We can too easily get lost in the "old stories". Can anyone relate to the following statements? "It always happens to me. I have such a hard life!" Dare to be different and make a choice to look for solutions, asking yourself "What have I got to lose?" You will be amazed at the outcome of making a different choice and mustering up the courage to give it a go!

One of the many memories I have is when I sustained an injury at work which resulted in having to undergo major surgery on my arms, leaving nerve damage, loss of feeling, weakness and some loss in the use of my arms. On top of that I lost my job and my employers put me on a disability pension. This was devastating to me—I was so physically fit and independent. I spent a long time in victim consciousness, feeling very sorry for myself and angry and experiencing feelings of grief and loss. Strangely enough, it turned out to be one of the most profound turning points in my life. Two years later my life began to change and I started a wonderful journey of self-discovery. When unpleasant things happen in our lives we can tend to complain and feel sorry for ourselves. It's not always clear to see that these times are, in reality, a gift of much-needed change.

From my own experience and working with clients, scarcity and lack are two things that prevent us from experiencing abundance in our lives. If we worry about our finances and what we can't afford, this reflects our state of scarcity.

Questions to ponder

- Was your family living with scarcity?
- Could your family only afford the bare necessities?
- Were you introduced to money by the experience of your parents and other family members?
- Did your family create abundance or lack (and therefore, scarcity) in their lives?

Affirmation

Money flows in my life. I am prosperous.

Budgeting and Saving

In society today there is a definite stigma about people who are in financial difficulties. The repercussions of this stigma can cause feelings of failure and embarrassment. Some suffer and worry in private trying to figure out how to resolve the situation. Some try to avoid and deny it by not opening bills or even hiding them. Financial difficulties can cause many problems. We can feel helpless and don't know where we can turn to next.

As many of us know, these circumstances can become overwhelming and can quickly spiral out of control as we are forced to look at resolving our financial issues. There are always solutions and there are also consequences for taking action. We worry and we struggle to survive which can all too easily lead to stress and sometimes illness (physical and/or mental). Relationships can breakdown affecting our families and friendships. As I have mentioned earlier, facing our financial problems right from the start can bring resolution without causing undue stress.

Why do we need to budget? It's important to keep track of where your money goes so you don't live beyond your means.

One way to keep track of your spending is to match your budget with your bank statement. It's important that you see the money coming into your bank account as well as the money going out. Use both your transaction account and credit card statements to see if your budget truly reflects your spending.

Keep a diary and write down what you spend in a notebook and take it with you at all times. Include your groceries, newspapers, snacks,

morning coffee, clothes, shoes, bus tickets, restaurants and movie tickets. If you don't want to keep a diary, simply hold onto your receipts, but do remember to include items that don't require a receipt, such as contributing to a staff farewell gift, etc.

A budget is a guide that tracks your financial direction and growth.

A budget is used to assist you to be in control of your finances

It is a tool you can use for measuring your financial progress and is an aid to achieving your goals. You may have goals and dreams, but if you don't set up guidelines for reaching them and you don't measure your progress, how will you know where you are headed?

A budget lets you control your money instead of your money controlling you.

Instead of your money controlling you a budget puts you control of your money.

A budget will inform you and let you know you are living within your means. Before credit cards became a popular way of buying things using cash to for your everyday purchases enabled you to determine if you were living within your means because you had money left over after paying all your bills.

A budget can help you meet your saving goals. It includes a mechanism for setting aside money for savings and investments.

Following a realistic budget frees up spare cash so you can spend your money on things that really matter, instead of frittering it away on things you don't even remember buying.

A budget helps your entire family focus on common goals.

A budget helps you prepare for emergencies or large unanticipated expenses.

A budget can be used to improve your personal relationships. It is a tool you and your partner can use to develop a greater understanding of your financial situation. A budget can be used to assist you as you work together to achieve your goals. A budget reveals areas where you are spending too much money so you can focus on your most important goals. You will be surprised to find that you will argue less about money with these steps in place.

A budget can keep you out of debt or help you get out of debt.

A budget actually creates extra money for you.

A budget helps you sleep better at night because you don't lie awake worrying about how you are going to make ends meet.

Go to the A Spiritual Budget website and download an Income and Expenditure Statement. **www.aspiritualbudget.com**

Choose a timeframe for your budget aligned to your pay cycle.

- Weekly guide;
- Fortnightly guide; or
- Monthly guide

Assessing your income

The first section of the budget sheet records your total income for the week/fortnight/month. Remember to record all your expenses.

Assessing your expenses

Next, enter your (weekly/fortnightly/monthly) expenses. Include eating out, hobbies, cigarettes, takeaways, gifts, pharmaceuticals, petrol, alcohol, utility bills, rent, mortgages and other large expenses. Remember to include credit card payments and personal loans.

Working out the difference

When you have completed your income and expenditure statement, you can clearly see how much regular income you receive and where your money is spent. Subtract your total expenses from your total income to arrive at your net result. Do this in the last part of your budget.

Tweaking your budgeting plan

- Have you correctly converted income and expenditure to the time frame you are using?
- Is the result what you were expecting?
- Does your budget show you are spending more than you earn?
- Do you find yourself reaching for your credit card?
- What can you do to change your budget?
- Is it time to make achievable financial goals?

Until you become confident that you are in control of your weekly/fortnightly/monthly budget, complete a new budget statement each payday. It will ensure you stay in control and help stop unnecessary spending. If you "blow your budget" in one pay period, try to make a temporary adjustment in the next week to bring the dollars back on track.

Keeping it current

Keep track of your expenses. Review your budget plans every couple of months, or when your circumstances change. For example:

- If you start, lose or change your job
- If you receive a pay rise or pay reduction
- If you move house
- If your marital status changes
- If you start a family

How budgeting will improve your life

Until you become confident that you are in control of your weekly/fortnightly/monthly budget, complete a new budget statement each payday. It will ensure you stay in control and help stop unnecessary spending. If you "blow your budget" in one pay period, try to make a temporary adjustment in the next week to bring the dollars back on track.

Keep it up to date

Keep track of your expenses. Review your budget plans every couple of months, or when your circumstances change. For example:

- If you start, lose or change your job
- If you receive a pay rise or pay reduction
- If you move house
- If your marital status changes
- If you start a family

Adjust your budget according to your circumstances.

Chapter 3

I Am Who I Choose to Be

"Our deepest fear is not that we are inadequate. Our deepest fear is that we are powerful beyond measure. It is our light, not our darkness, that most frightens us. We ask ourselves, 'Who am I to be brilliant, gorgeous, talented and fabulous?' Actually, who are you not to be? . . . . We are all meant to shine . . . ."

Marianne Williamson

Step 2 of A Spiritual Budget is Gratitude, Self-Acceptance and Self Worth

How much abundance we experience in life stems from our belief systems and the limitations we place on ourselves. Most of this behaviour is imprinted on us from a very young age.

Our self-esteem is very much a part of how we experience abundance in our life. If we have high self-esteem we have confidence and the ability to be whatever and whoever we choose. Our self-worth is very strong and we trust and follow our inner feelings to lead us in the right direction.

If our self-esteem is low we have low self-worth. We look away from self to others for approval. We want to be accepted and loved and we want to fit in. We often feel rejected and find we don't feel complete inside. Why do you think this is? In many cases it's because we don't know how to listen and trust our inner voice and we don't feel safe being in our own skin. As we explore and get to know and understand ourselves much more, we become aware that we are more than we could have ever imagined.

Life is a journey encompassing many experiences. The most important part of getting to a destination is the journey itself. This starts from the day we are born and each new day is an experience. Every little step takes us to another place to experience and grow.

We firstly learn how to eat, speak and walk and at that young age every day is an adventure. Those who cared for and loved us did the best they could from their own life experiences. Each person's journey is unique and our experiences make us who we are today.

We remember our childhood in so many different ways. At times we remember the happiness and at other times we remember the pain. Love is an interesting subject to explore and how we interpret love differs from one individual to the next. From a young age confusion begins as to what love really is. When we are young we are very sensitive and as children we take on our parents challenges, as if they are our own. We love our parents no matter who or what they are.

I experienced abandonment and rejection from the age of eight when my parents separated and my father went his way and my mother left us for another man. My brother and I only had each other and I started caring for him when we were left with family who didn't really love or care for us. What I find truly remarkable is how we still loved, not only each other, but our parents and the ones caring for us. Children have such resilience.

My brother and I would hold hands and share stories and dream how our mum was coming back to get us, to take us away and love us again. Children believe what they are told by the ones they love and trust the most and even if they are let down, they still hold hope that they will be loved, wanted and nurtured.

Some of us grow up and become bitter and resentful, blaming our parents for how and why our lives are the way they are. This only serves to make us a victim to life. We judge our families and we judge ourselves and from this belief we can create a similar life for ourselves. I have experienced this myself and heard this many times from clients.

Life has made me who I am today. I learned to endure, to keep going and I never gave up.

Looking back at my parents (who grew up in alcoholic families with emotional and physical abuse) I now know that they didn't know any other way to be. They gave in to what they believed about themselves and that which they had learnt from their parents, teachers, peers, religion and society. They didn't know that they could step beyond self-imposed judgements and limitations and grow into their potential by being much more than they ever dreamed possible.

In my 20s I came to the realisation that I was not the 'genetic mess' my parents were. I learnt that I could break the cycle and make different choices. Our genetics are so much more than what we see in our parents and in our families. There is so much to explore and learn about who we really are. We can change and recreate ourselves and have the relationships we have dreamed of and the jobs we have always wanted.

Working with students and clients, I see many people who show absolutely no gratitude or appreciation in their lives and this, too, is learned behaviour. They are lost and feel life is hard and unfair. They are living in the past and have become victims to life and they have a false sense of entitlement ("the world owes me"). This is not the case, for our life is what we make it—we are not owed a thing. We create that we are poor, unloved and unable to fit in. The sooner we learn to understand this process (and act on it), the sooner life will begin to change.

Attitude is a big part of how we live our life and by making adjustments to our attitude in a more positive way, we bring about change. We create our own reality by our thoughts and we don't realise that by thinking negative thoughts, we stay the same. For example, if you repeatedly affirm "no one will help me" and you hold onto this belief, this will be your experience. There are many people who would love to help you. The key to this is very simple—you have to take responsibility and not be a victim to life. To this and help will arrive. Positive affirmation: "The right circumstances and the right people are already here and will show up on time." This really works and with a positive change in your attitude, you will be surprised how much easier life will flow.

Our parents sometimes try to shape us in their own image and this is when it becomes a challenge to the child. In most instances the child will give in and try to 'be' their parents. They can do this through fear or they can do this so they are lovable and as a means of 'fitting in'. By behaving this way, children do not discover who they really are—they simply identify that they are their parents. It is sad that at this young age children aren't encouraged to grow and be their own self. I spent most of my life not knowing who I was and feeling inferior to everyone. I didn't feel I was intelligent or that I was capable of achieving anything. Of course, this was simply learned behaviour and far from the truth. Despite all this, I feel gratitude for the learning experience this offered me and for the knowledge that I am so much more and will continue to grow and step into my potential.

With the power of choice, I chose to learn from my own childhood experiences, rather than to repeat them. As such, my partner and I raised our children in a loving and caring environment.

When we look back at our youth, we can sometimes see life as a cruel place and through this experience we have judged harshly. Yet in our young hearts we were enriched with the experience of whatever came our way. If we endure and have the courage to keep going, our lenses are clear and we see the truth of how things really are. If we blame and feel we are a victim to life, the lenses in our eyes become clouded and we see this cloudiness all around us. It doesn't matter who and what our parents were, we see it all through cloudiness. This is the journey and what we learned along the way. There is no "right or wrong" or "should or shouldn't" and it is never, ever too late to explore and understand more of who we are.

Here are some questions to ponder. Please allow yourself to feel without judgement:

- Can you look back on your life and feel gratitude?
- How much do you value yourself?
- Do you have compassion and understanding for your parents or the ones who raised you?
- What was the experience of growing up for you?
- What were your best memories?
- What were your worst memories?

- What did you learn from the experience?
- How have you parented your children?

Positive affirmations:

- I am worthy and deserving of abundance and love.
- I love who I am and all that I do. I love and accept myself exactly as I am now.
- I am more than what has happened to me.
- I am who I choose to be!

Chapter 4

Grief and Loss

*When your fear touches someone's pain,
it becomes pity. When your love touches
someone's pain, it becomes compassion."*

Stephen Levine

Step 3 of a Spiritual Budget is Hope and Adaptability

Every day I work with people experiencing financial grief and loss, caused by many different circumstances. What always amazes me is how the spirit in human form endures the path of its chosen life's journey.

Grief and loss can take many forms—the most acknowledged being the death of a loved one. Other types of grief and loss are separation, divorce, unemployment, loss of business, illness, disability, domestic violence and other types of abuse, as well as retirement and loss of the family home. All of these losses can lead to financial difficulty leaving individuals and families feeling vulnerable and not knowing where to turn to next.

Grief and loss in marriage difficulties (separation and divorce) are not generally acknowledged as a death, but they do nevertheless represent great loss for all family members. The grief experienced by family members following relationship difficulties is very real. In the case of a separation, the reality for many is that they may be facing financial difficulty. They could possibly lose the family home and children may have to change schools and make new friendships.

There may be grief and loss surrounding parental access when children can often find themselves shuffled between homes. The children's access to their grandparents and other family members can also be lost. Parents may be too busy with financial and legal matters to notice or respond to their own grief, let alone the grief their children may be experiencing.

Another example of grief and loss can be in the form of being a business owner. Many of us have a dream to start a business. We borrow money, we put our homes and everything we own 'in hock' to establish the business. The business can start well, but then adversity can throw a spanner in the works in any number of ways—the rent can double or business can simply slow down. We work long hours, but don't have a wage to take home, our credit cards are maxed out, we get behind with our mortgage or we can't make our car payment. The bills don't get paid and creditors ring continuously. This happens all too often in small businesses and the consequences can be devastating. The grieving and the loss associated with these factors can affect us in all areas of our lives.

Grieving is a natural process that needs to be felt and acknowledged. All of us, at some stage in our lives, go through grief in its various forms and we each express ourselves in a unique way throughout this process. Remember, with the loss of anything in our lives, it is important that we 'experience' (acknowledge and feel) the grief.

Grief is real and sometimes a little help can open doors. Don't be afraid to ask for help if you feel stuck in your emotions.

It is a well-documented fact that suppressed grief can be the cause of both physical and mental illness. As a part of the healing process we need to express the grief and we need to acknowledge the loss we are feeling. Our responses may depend on our feelings about the loss, our state of health at the time, the implications of the loss, the assessment of the loss, our interpretation of the events surrounding the loss, or whether or not the loss was anticipated. It may have been an isolated loss or part of a chain of losses. Irrespective of how the loss is manifested, we need to acknowledge the grief in order for us to be able to move on.

Grief and loss can affect our moods and behaviours and it is of great benefit if we ourselves (and the people around us) accept this is as a normal part of the grieving process. Some of us try to 'fix' people going through the grieving process by attempting to make them feel better, telling them to be strong and that they should just keep on going. Who is this for? Is it for them or is it for you because you have not felt your own grief from the past? Allow the people you love to be who they are and if this upsets you, use this opportunity to feel your own losses.

We may have experienced a lot of grief in our lives—even the death of a family pet as a child causes grief. It could be a relationship break up, being separated from our parents, or the loss of friends. We are told to 'suck it up' and to be tough. Sucking it up and being tough doesn't allow us to actually experience the grieving process as the feelings just get brushed over. We suppress what we couldn't handle and then wonder why we get sick.

There comes a time in our lives when we just can't hold on any more. It can take the smallest of events to trigger a reaction. Then, what we have suppressed for so long bubbles up to the surface and the grief that was buried so deep within comes spilling out. All that we have not owned or acknowledged during those times overflows. We feel we will never experience the joy of life again.

This is when the grief that we have suppressed into our body can manifest as physical illness or we may develop mental illness because we were unable to cope with the amount of suppressed grief from that very deep place within. We haven't learnt to feel as we feel without judgment, nor do we experience acceptance from those around us because we have all been taught that it's not OK to express our emotions. With this belief, how can we ever feel safe in our experience? What we have been trained to do is to think our way out of feeling by distracting ourselves with our ever-busy minds.

The deep grief that I remember (as I have discussed in an earlier chapter where I had been not wanted as a young child and given away) has affected me the most of all my life experiences. The feelings of not being wanted, being replaced and not being good enough can plague us throughout our lives.

The only way that I could get through my experience was to truly allow myself to grieve and to let go, because the tighter I hung onto 'it's not fair' or I blamed others for my feelings, the only person I was hurting was myself and I became a victim to life.

I have learnt that I must always allow myself to feel and accept life in whatever way it presents to really have 'the knowing' that my reactions are a choice. I choose to be the champion, the warrior, who takes life in their stride and never gives up. This is how we transform fear into love. We take life in, we feel it, acknowledge it and make a loving choice to be kind and accepting to self. With this change in attitude we can only have success.

**Grief and loss is not just about death—
it's about changes in our lives and our
expectations.**

There is another type of grief I would like to
discuss with you, which you may never consider
to be a loss. When we have the opportunity to
step up and grow into our success, we can feel
grief for what we are losing as we step into the
new. We are sad about the friends and family
we will be leaving behind, yet it can also be a
most wondrous journey into the unknown for
those who have the courage to experience life
to the full.

There is another side to this I would like to
have you contemplate. How many times have
we had the opportunity to change our lives
and yet we have chosen to stay where we are
because we are comfortable with the old and
uncomfortable with the thought of stepping
into the unknown? It takes strong self-esteem

and courage to keep moving forward and to not look behind. I believe that courage is contagious. The more you muster up the courage to step out into the unknown and trust, the easier it becomes.

Sometimes our families and friends discourage us from being our best because they have not achieved their best. Can you identify with that? I know I can. Quite often we don't get acceptance of our grief from others. I haven't always felt supported in my personal growth by family or friends. Through my own life's journey, feeling is truly living and if you want to experience a new way, find a mentor or a teacher who can take you on a journey of self-discovery.

So the grieving process can truly be a gift if we allow ourselves to let go of what we once knew and of what we believed we were. When we let go this opens doors and allows for new beginnings.

In my wildest dreams I never imagined I could write a book and be who I am today. It's because of what I have experienced through my journey that I am who I am now. We are more than our genetic inheritance. We do not have to become what we are told to become or what our thinking limits us to be. Every single one of us is so much more than we dare imagine. I am living proof that the process of self-discovery opens doors to a joyful and fulfilling life. It's all a choice. Do you have the courage to change and step into a new and joyful way of life? If I can do it, so can you.

Feel into the grief and loss in your life and how you dealt with it. If you're stuck in your emotions through the grieving process, don't be afraid to ask for help. It could be a small step that will make all the difference to how you are in the moment. Have the courage to leave the old behind and consider taking that one small step at a time.

Questions to ponder:

- Where do you call home? Is it a physical place or a state of mind?
- Are you more comfortable with your family or your extended family?
- Where do you feel safe, where you can be yourself?
- Where are you holding onto the past or not letting go of the past?
- Are you ready to let go?
- Can you visualise an open door? It's your choice. If you want to step through, but can't, what is stopping you?

Affirmations

- I choose love, I choose to heal.
- I choose to accept and love myself.
- Let there be peace on Earth and let it begin with me.
- I accept what I cannot change.

- I now do unto others, as I would have them do unto me.
- I now have compassion, even for those I do not understand.
- I treasure every day I am living.
- My life has value and others appreciate who I am.

Chapter 5

Resistance

"People don't resist change. They resist being changed."

Peter M. Senge

Step 4 of a Spiritual Budget involves the qualities of courage, persistence and self-determination.

Resistance is a part of life—everyone encounters it. Breaking through resistance is as simple as taking that first step. Just as athletes encounter resistance when they are training for a big event—increasing their fitness and muscle strength—there is going to be some soreness and some irritability as you tread this necessary path.

We looked at the resistance of paying bills and not being financially responsible for our financial situations. What belief systems do we have in place that convince us that we are less than who we truly are? How does this play out limiting and holding us back from having the job we have always wanted and the relationships we have always dreamed of? How does this stop us from embracing our true potential?

$ = what? We need to face the truth of what money means to us. I came to the realisation that money is just paper and it's of great concern to me that the world is ruled so much by money. Let's look at money as an energy we exchange for our wants and needs.

Excuses some people give for why they are haven't found success include: 'I can't afford it, I can't be any more than this, I am not good enough, I will never get that job that pays well'. There are many excuses why we don't do well in life. We listen to the words of our parents, teachers and peers. We believed what they told us about ourselves to be true. That belief and that heavy feeling in your heart of *'can't'* is how resistance can affect us. We don't want to see how we are handling our finances, so we make up excuses why we can't be successful, keeping ourselves small and locked firmly in the systems of government, religion and society that control us.

Many of us work hard for this energy we call money. Have you ever done an income and expenditure of this energy you receive for all your hard work and assessed how you spend it? Take note of how much money has passed through your hands over your whole lifetime.

How does this make you feel? Do you feel a twinge inside and a reluctance to know? You want your life to improve, yet you resist from putting everything on the table and facing the truth.

Maybe you have been responsible, saved and spent your money wisely. Maybe you haven't. Even if you haven't been wise with your money, you can always start from this very moment to change. We might have resistances with money. Let's look at the truth in all aspects of our life. How did we learn to be resistant to change, to having that great job or being the best we can be?

Resistance is a habit we learnt in childhood. When a child, for example, is given a chore or something they don't want to do they create ways to avoid it—they resist and throw tantrums or even hide to get out of doing the chore. Can you remember the excuses you made to get out of doing what you were supposed to do, that which you found difficult? If you failed, were you afraid of the consequences? I have seen this in my own children and grandchildren. It's a way of life and so very common in our society. Our parents could have been the same, so this is learnt behaviour. I wish I could have been as aware as I am now when my children were young. I would have encouraged them to face all their fears and to do their best from a very young age.

How about as an adult? Do we still run those patterns when we want to avoid and deny what needs to be done, to achieve and be our very best? What are we afraid of? Maybe it's a fear of being exposed or we might lose face for what we don't know or what we don't have. Is this really doing our best? When we do our best there can only be success.

Some of us will resist in order to avoid confrontation. We try to make peace with the situation, so we don't have to face or feel what's really going on or how we really feel, so we avoid and compromise ourselves. We are afraid to 'make waves'. It is much more comfortable for things to stay the same.

I had to face the truth and look at where I was at. As soon as I got close to success, the old sabotage patterns and behaviours emerged. I felt criticised, that I wasn't good enough and I blamed others, when really it was my own avoidance, denial and sabotage patterns that I had created to keep me small. Once I stopped blaming others, believing it was everyone else's fault and brought it back to myself, everything changed. I simply faced the truth of what was happening and looked at what I had created to stop myself from succeeding.

The resistance I am feeling while writing this book is crushing at times and all those negative beliefs I have in myself have come up to hinder the progress of the book. What I have learnt is to keep going and never give up. Pushing through resistance has boundless rewards.

Most of my life I went out of my way to not upset people and as a result of that behaviour, I became a doormat. In essence, I was allowing my soul to be trampled on. I have changed now and I have found my voice. I have learnt to use resistance as a guiding light to show me the direction I need to take. Whenever I feel the pressure of "I can't" or those old beliefs come up, I keep going and I don't give up. This has changed my life and, yes, it is a challenge at times, but as I have said many times in this book—when we don't give up, there can only be success.

Other times we rely too much on what others think and we can't even use our own thoughts. We rely on what others think and do to help us succeed. We want others to do and fix things for us.

Life is so incredibly difficult when we are not being honest or complete in self. We need to have a good look at ourselves and move past the old way that we think we should be.

Low self-esteem is giving into our resistance of excelling and living our potential—believing what we know to be true within us. It is more comfortable and easy to be in resistance—staying in that relationship which is over, being resistant to letting go of our house, or a way of life, or being safe. We choose to live in misery because we are afraid to change.

Until we have 'the knowing' and the courage to face our problems and deal with them directly and accept ourselves for who and what we are, avoidance and denial will hinder us. We can change by 'feeling and stepping' into the resistance, the truth of the experience—without judgment. It's uplifting and encouraging to notice that the confused feeling of going around in circles slowly disappears. We only have to give it a try and to know we are not perfect and never will be. We simply need to be understanding and accepting of ourselves. Perfection is learning from our mistakes.

Can you imagine if we embraced resistance as a friend? Those feelings and excuses we make—'I can't, I'm not smart enough, I haven't got it in me, I'm too young, I'm too old'—imagine how different our life, our world would be if we were taught how to face the feelings of resistance at a young age. We wouldn't be resisting and throwing tantrums and we wouldn't be afraid of the consequences of being wrong, or of getting into trouble for what we didn't know.

Do you think children are the only ones who have this behaviour? I have encountered people, both in my professional and personal life, who run and hide from the truth or from the problems in their lives. They live in illusion and they are afraid of change. Sometimes they hold onto so much pain that if they faced the truth, it would take them far out of their comfort zone. It all becomes too hard, and so it's easier to be miserable with what they know, instead of stepping into a new way of being.

We can push a button and reset ourselves on the path of facing our resistance, embracing our problems and fears and resolving them by

doing our very best in each and every moment. The key is to love the truth and to be OK with ourselves. This takes courage and the rewards are immeasurable. To discipline ourselves is vital to stepping up and leaving resistance behind. As we continually face our fears and feel safe, it becomes easier and we feel more complete and contented in all aspects of our lives, including our finances.

We are much more than just our behaviour. When we are out to please others, to get their approval, we become resentful and we don't feel happy within ourselves. We have to be determined to bring about change within ourselves. By doing this, we learn to be whole and contented and life becomes much more enjoyable.

So can you see when we face our fears and walk towards resistance and embrace the truth, all aspects of our life expand? We see that we are constantly growing in our relationships, our finances and our successes.

Keep a resistance journal. Be aware of how often you feel resistance and whether or not you give in. If you do choose to step through, make sure that you genuinely acknowledge your courage for taking that step.

Questions:

- How often do you feel resistance?
- Do you have the courage to face your fear and do your very best?

Affirmations

- I am courageous and face my fears.
- I take everything in my stride and keep going.
- I keep walking, I don't look back and I do not stop.
- I allow the courage in my heart to overcome any fear I feel.

Chapter 6

Speaking Up

"The world is a dangerous place, not because of those who do evil, but because of those who look on and do nothing"

Albert Einstein

Step 5 of A Spiritual Budget is about embracing our uniqueness and learning to speak up for ourselves.

Many of us keep so much within and the thought of speaking up brings up all manner of feeling and fears. We compromise ourselves. It is a feeling of another knowing more and being more capable than we think we are.

In the area of our finances it is also a fact that some people don't speak up (for example, not letting banks and finance companies know when we are experiencing financial difficulties) and this brings consequences. If you speak up and be honest about your situation, there are always solutions to the problem. If we don't speak up, we suffer from avoidance and denial, we have anxiety and we become depressed. I find that many clients judge their circumstances. They are embarrassed because they are struggling due to their financial difficulty.

Money is the tip of the iceberg. What's below the surface? Suppressing our feelings and being afraid to express how we feel can be a most painful experience. We can feel tongue-tied or anxious about our finances. How we are in all aspects of our life is depicted by how much money we do or do not have. We can either be too giving or be taken advantage of. We might be mean or we might simply begrudge giving or spending anything. Or for some people it can be a way of getting their own way or having control. It's important to remember that money is just metal coins and pieces of paper and that our true worth is more to do with valuing and feeling worthy in our own selves.

Why do we have problems with speaking up? For the most part, it is a symptom of childhood and that part of us that was afraid to speak up for fear of criticism. Take the inner child, for example. When we have a trauma in our young lives, there is a part of us that can remain the same age as when the trauma took place. In other words, that part of us does not mature. For example, if at the age of six you were blamed for something you didn't do and you suffered physically and emotionally as a consequence, this may well have caused you trauma. So, as an adult if you are blamed for something you didn't do, your response can come from the age of that six year old—that part of you that has not matured.

How we were listened to by our parents, clergy, teachers and society had a great impact on us as well. As young children we wanted to express ourselves. We were full of life and love and sometimes this could have been met with resistance and the ones we loved and trusted the most may have responded negatively. This could have taken any number of verbal forms:

- You think you're so smart
- Little boys/girls should be seen and not heard
- That's the craziest thing I've ever heard
- What do you know?
- Not now, I'm busy (*what you have to say isn't important*)

- Who told you that? (*scepticism*)
- Don't say such a thing
- I don't believe you
- You better not talk like that
- God will punish you for saying/thinking that
- That's not a nice thing to say
- That's not true
- You're stupid
- What a crazy idea
- You don't make any sense
- You think you're so smart
- You're crazy

Can you feel how crushing this experience would have been for a child who was so excited about sharing an experience or story?

From my own experience as a child I was told repeatedly to go outside because 'children should be seen and not heard'. I was told I was stupid and dumb. Understandably, this had an impact on me. I felt I had nothing worthwhile to offer or say and that no-one would want to listen to me. I felt I didn't matter.

From this experience we form a belief that we are "not good enough" or that we are bad or we are wrong. This is imprinted and hard-wired in our brain. We carry this belief into adolescence and eventually into adulthood, like so many self-defeating and self-sabotaging beliefs we form at a young age. So our beliefs about ourselves are that we are not important and what we have to say is not important.

We create in ourselves a self-image, a self-concept or an identity that we are not creditable, smart or intelligent. So, we look away from ourselves for approval. We look for someone stronger to prop us up because we feel inadequate within ourselves. Whilst we have a fear of consequences (there are consequences for everything in life), there are also consequences for not taking action. We worry what people think.

How sad it is that society values the opinions of others, but all too often we don't value our own self. We wait for people to validate who we are, how we look and what we say. This is a tortuous way of being. A way to move past this is self-acceptance of who you are in each and every moment.

Not speaking up can be identified in many ways. We may remain quiet at meetings, or in awkward situations we say nothing for fear of the consequences of speaking up. If we do say something and it doesn't get the response we wanted, we can often feel angry—almost as if we weren't heard at all. We can justify not speaking up by saying that we didn't know enough or that we didn't have the right information, but this only serves to make us angry and we feel insignificant, stupid and frustrated and we don't have a good sense of ourselves.

We bring all this to ourselves by having fear, worrying and comparing ourselves to others, worrying what they think of us and whether or not we are accepted. This is all our own self-judgment and there is absolutely no cause to blame others.

Why didn't I speak up? I've given this a lot of thought. When I was young I can't remember feeling validated and I certainly can't remember anyone ever speaking up for me, which is yet another example of learnt behaviour. I learnt not to speak up for myself, that I wasn't worthy of speaking up for myself.

This problem in society explains why the bullies have their way more often than not. It is why the Earth is in the chaos it is in and why so many people get away with so much and why we wait in line for 'a pittance of a life'. We feel at times we are only one person. How could we possibly make a difference? These are simply excuses for keeping us small.

Be uplifted in the knowledge that you can make a difference. Do your best and be the best you can be and don't be afraid to be heard. That's all it takes and all anyone can ask of you. Speaking up and standing up for what we feel to be just and fair takes courage, but it brings great reward.

It is also important to work on negative energy and emotions and understand that we must not limit ourselves. It takes courage to be our authentic self, to know that we do have a voice and the wisdom to be our true self, rather than who we have been told to be.

We often feel we cannot support our own thoughts without someone else's thoughts to back us up. We can never compare ourselves with anyone. We are all unique and have our own gifts and so much to offer when we are being our true selves.

Not speaking up is common in our society. We need to break down the barriers of fear and allow the passion for life to fill our hearts with the meaning of love. Sadly, some will not believe they are capable of such wonder. They push against walls, rather than having the courage to break them down to see the newness within the journey of self-discovery—a journey that takes them well beyond the confines of society and especially religion.

What stops us from speaking up? The most logical answer is fear.

We see fear and suppression often in the community—people playing small and not standing up to be counted. We are kept down and controlled by the church, society and establishments. To allow change to happen we must firstly change ourselves. If we change and become more who we truly are, everything changes around us. Don't just take my word for it, try it yourself. There is nothing to lose. Contemplate how you can step up and live in a new way and open yourself up to success.

Each and every day practice speaking up. Learn to trust that as an individual you have something worthwhile to contribute. If you don't feel comfortable doing this and negative thoughts such as "I shouldn't have said that" enter your head, push those thoughts aside understanding that this is self-judgement. This is a wonderful opportunity to acknowledge your feelings and to make a new choice to feel patient with yourself, as your confidence grows.

When we are afraid to speak up, this is resistance, as we outlined in an earlier chapter. It represents a place in us that is limited by the fear of living, hoping that nothing upsets our days so we can quietly get on with what we do without any conflict or fear of being confronted, keeping everything in a controlled, quiet way. Do you truly feel you will grow living like this? It's like being numb inside. It stifles our creativity, our fun and joy in life. All we need to do is simply learn how to respond without fear and to feel our value and worth. This is the place where we speak the clearest and brightest.

Being in the state of reacting (getting upset and not feeling heard) only serves to justify our fear-based behaviour. Don't be afraid of being successful and do stop worrying what others say. If more people spoke up, the world would be a better place. Stand up and be counted and see the difference it makes.

Let the wonders of the universe move you beyond your wildest dreams.

Be kind and be an example of giving in the most loving way.

Have courage and look beyond the confines of all around you.

Task

Every evening sit down quietly and review your day. Be honest with yourself and re-write the main events of the day in a new way. Take note of when you did speak up and when you didn't. This way you can 're-write' instances in a new way where you did speak up. This is an empowering process that teaches us to identify and changes our behaviours.

Affirmations

- The miracle I seek is me
- I am a powerful agent of change
- I do and am my best in each and every moment
- I speak my truth with confidence

Chapter 7

Giving and Receiving

"Kindness in words creates confidence. Kindness in thinking creates profoundness. Kindness in giving creates Love."

Lao Tsu

Step 6 of A Spiritual Budget is embracing kindness and giving. When you can learn to give, your life will be changed forever.

You will soon begin to seek out more and more opportunities of ways to give.

Giving opens us up for more possibilities. It is only when we give we can truly receive. We live in a society of always wanting more, where nothing is ever enough. When we live life in this way it becomes all about me, me, me and my needs. With this way of thinking and being, the gift of giving is lost.

When we are on the path of self-discovery we soon learn (when giving openly from a heart-filled place) that we are far from wanting, owning and having expectations that are imposed upon us by society.

Of course, there is the cheerful giver who gives from the heart without any expectation of return. This act of kindness can only bring joy into your life and the lives of others.

There is a belief dynamic that many run in differing degrees. We can become very needy and try to please others. I know this dynamic well as I ran it myself for many years. We don't necessarily have the awareness that we are behaving in this way. What we do feel is the deep pain of rejection.

Some of us in our earlier life did experience rejection and it stayed with us through childhood, adolescence and into adulthood. We crave to be loved, accepted and to fit in with family, friends and work mates. Our self-esteem is very low and we feel a gut-wenching tug inside every time we think we have done the wrong thing or when we feel we are not appreciated for all we are and what we do for others.

Our motives are unclear and become tainted with fear. This is the dynamic of the fear of intimacy when everything in life is about others. It is a distorted way of thinking that we are a giver, when in reality we are being a pleaser.

If we do not like who we are, we feel neither confident nor comfortable in our own skin and we focus and project our thoughts and feelings away from ourselves to others. By doing this we attract people into our lives who use us, so we can feel needed.

We then start to feel resentful because we feel used. Guilt then builds up inside because we are taught to give and not look for gratitude. It turns out to be a vicious circle. I am aware I ran this dynamic and as I said, there are differing degrees. Let's just take a moment and ponder why we give and what our motives are. Perhaps you can relate to this resentment and guilt dynamic.

> *"We make a living by what we get, but we make a life by what we give"*
>
> Winston Churchill

I recently went to listen to two speakers—one is a well-known musician and singer from the past who works with youth and the other a producer and journalist who, while riding a pushbike, was hit by a car and suffered brain injury as a result of the accident.

The first speaker talked about his childhood and the focus on his talk was all about how difficult life was for him and how he was a survivor. It was all about him and nothing else. He was not giving—he was taking. He was looking for sympathy and wanting the audience to feel sorry for him. He succeeded in that mission, but I felt he gave absolutely nothing. He took for himself. The question is did I learn how to understand working with youth? No, I didn't. My experience of the talk was listening to a story that he told over and over again for his own healing.

The second speaker was truly inspirational. He gave a talk on the subject of brain injury. He spoke very little about himself and his attainments and after reading about him we discovered there were many more achievements. He only shared about himself when it was necessary. He openly taught us how we can identify, understand and assist brain injury clients. I felt inspired by his presentation and it gave me a clearer picture of an area in which I was not educated. So, as a result of the second speaker's presentation, I now have far more compassion and understanding of how to work with clients who have suffered brain injury.

May I ask you who was a giver and who was a taker? The first speaker thought he was doing a good job. In reality, was he? No, he wasn't. The second speaker was much more authentic and humble and he gave of himself open-heartedly.

When dealing with people we must be aware of their motives. Some are simply smooth talkers and it's because of these people that so many companies and undesirable characters try to scam and cheat us out of our hard-earned savings. It is the payday lenders and the undesirables of our community who pretend to give and do not have our interests at heart.

> *"I don't think you ever stop giving. I really don't. I think it's an on-going process. And it's not just about being able to write a check. It's being able to touch somebody's life".*

> Oprah Winfrey

When we learn to give from our hearts, we open ourselves to prosperity and it's not just about money. It's about getting on with life and experiencing giving what you can from a place of openness and joy.

What we think about the most creates our reality. Believing that your needs are not met and believing that you don't have 'this or that' are thoughts that will sabotage your quality of life. Even if opportunity does knock, we don't see it and we therefore allow ourselves to fall into the trap of lack.

What you think about will determine your reality. I can't speak for material riches, but I can speak of the opposite. If your thoughts are always on lack (lack of respect, lack of love, lack of money), then lack will always be a part of who you are.

One of the best things about giving is that it is never about us. It is about giving a part of ourselves, whether it is of a monetary nature or of our time. When giving comes from the heart, it gives us the opportunity to move away from ourselves and to give the gift of unconditional love in the best way we can. The reward is great and from this space of giving, we can embrace receiving.

Two things I have learnt about giving are its sacredness and its purity. In the past if someone gave me a gift, I was embarrassed and didn't want to accept it. What I have now learnt is that this was not being humble and didn't allow another the opportunity to give.

Task

Examine your motives for why you give.

Questions

- Are you needy?
- How does giving make you feel?
- Is it easy for you to receive?

Affirmations

- I choose to radiate success and love everywhere I go
- I choose to give the best of myself in everything I do
- I give and receive freely
- I am giving and compassionate
- I surrender my heart to the universe

Chapter 8

The Beauty of Simplicity

"Life is really simple, but we insist on making it complicated"

Confucius

Step 7 of a Spiritual Budget is Living Life Simply

When we are deeply involved in the process of living life to it's fullest every day, we are being aware and accepting of whatever presents and we truly know that we are never given anything we can't handle.

Many of us walk around numb and unaware. We do the same thing day in and day out and tolerate living a life in a bid to only survive. We sit in front of our computers and games and turn the volume of life down to low so that we can escape into a world so far from the truth of what is really happening around us. We numb ourselves with alcohol and other addictions to dull our senses, so we don't have to feel how we really feel. From this we get a false sense of courage and well-being. Some of us eat to extreme excess to cover our emotions and to fill the emptiness.

Life is so challenging for many and my heart has a deep understanding of the ridiculously difficult expectations religion and society has put on us in these times and times gone by that complicate our everyday life. We have been told what we have to believe, how to dress, what we are allowed to say and how we must fit in to be socially accepted. It's no wonder we find life a challenge. I am not suggesting anti-social behaviour. I do, however, believe that the rules and regulations of society take us away from the gifts of our own individual expression as spirit in human form.

Whenever there is any turmoil in our lives, it affects our financial circumstances. This is where I see living simply as a great benefit. Having multiple credit cards and a mortgage and spending more than we earn is a recipe for disaster. In the event of job loss, we instantly face financial difficulty. When we buy with credit it does not belong to us until we pay the debt. There is nothing wrong with having life's little luxuries. The problem is how we go about it. Budgeting, setting goals, putting a little away each week are things in which the whole family can participate. That 'must have' item is much more appreciated by everyone when it's enjoyed without the fear of a credit card statement landing in the post.

Some who experience hard times use their credit cards to survive and pay off other credit cards. This is a dangerous exercise that causes great financial concern. This creates avoidance and denial and when the bills do come in (including a maxed-out credit card), we find ourselves owing thousands of dollars—a harsh reality that hits hard. It is well-known that financial problems cause stress and anxiety—not having the money to pay the bills or buy food for our families is a major stress factor.

It takes courage to live a life of simplicity

I have experienced many clients who have a false sense of entitlement and who are in heavy debt, yet they will not help themselves. They feel they have to live in an exclusive area, but that address comes with the price tag of going without food and having very little money to clothe and care for their families. However, they refuse to move to a less expensive area. Can you see how we can make life such a struggle to impress or to be seen a certain way? People have their choices and they choose their experiences. By keeping life simple we become grateful for everything we have and are humbled by the life experience we create on our journey.

I see many clients suppressed by the systems and have felt and experienced this through my own journey as well. We enter into relationships that are toxic because we have low self-worth and we give so much of ourselves trying to make things work. We compromise to keep the peace, even though we feel that deep, sinking feeling inside and every time we smooth things over we feel relief for only a little while. We do this time and time again. The truth of the matter is we are selling ourselves out.

In other instances we play small and are not truthful to save face, to fit in and to feel that we belong. We have forgotten that the only person to belong to is ourselves. We agree with others even though in our hearts we know that's not our truth. Imagine what it would be like to say, "No, that's not my reality. I don't need to agree or go along with you". Imagine having that truth deep inside of you.

It's quite sad that life seems to be mostly about wanting and that nothing is ever enough. "If I have that new TV or new car, I will be happy, I will feel better, I will feel accepted." This is totally learnt behaviour based on our distorted beliefs. Absolutely nothing away from us will ever fill the hole within. That feeling of contentment can only be found by self-discovery of the truth of who we truly are.

Can you see how complicated and hard life becomes when everything is about what others think, what we want and what we must have to fit in and be the same as others? When this happens, the gift of who we truly are is denied and forgotten.

Not only do we as adults struggle, our children go to school and have to fit into a box, which limits their individual expression. There are many types of intelligence and the school system does not cater for our little ones who do not fit in the boxes.

My young Granddaughter is very intelligent and sensitive and like many other children, she constantly battled with her schoolwork. It was found that she was having problems seeing in class sitting under a florescent light. The problem was rectified and now she is improving out of sight. This is just a small example how our children's individual needs to grow and expand can be neglected, which can debilitate or limit their learning potential.

One day I was going to a movie with a dear friend when two other friends came to visit and I allowed them to talk me out of my commitment to my friend. I cancelled and instantly had remorse for what I had done. I hurt my friend who later found out about it. To this day I still learn from that experience. It's so easy to just agree with another, to gossip, to be heard, to want to be liked, to be part of a crowd. This behaviour is far from the truth of our hearts, our knowing and our way of being.

I have run this pattern so much in my life, agreeing with others to be liked so that I would fit in. I sold myself out in my marriage. It wasn't my partner's fault—he is a very good and decent man—it was my own lack of self-worth, my own lack of self-value. I just went along with mostly everything because it was easier to agree, rather than to cause a fuss. I was simply living a lie. There was absolutely no truth in my living at all. How many of you can identify with compromising and selling yourself out?

I have had to acknowledge the injustice and pain I caused myself. It started at a young age as most of our behaviours do. We lie to get out of trouble. We have fears of not being liked or loved and we carry this into adolescence, then though to adulthood.

We can often think too much. From my personal experience, I have noticed that what I continuously think about actually becomes my reality. We can go over and over what has happened in the past or what someone has said to us or we can worry about what may happen in the future. Can you see how this complicates our lives? Our world is in our imagination and our thoughts and we can complicate our lives by over-thinking, which makes life difficult and wastes a lot of energy.

Living in the present simplifies our lives—this is awareness. Life becomes so much easier and we become grateful for what we have. We don't get caught up in the wants and needs, like so many around us. I have learnt to be and to do my best and to make a difference with little fuss, enjoying every one of life's challenges. This is the beautiful world of self-discovery.

When our lives are uncomplicated we are never lonely. We find a 'oneness' with all living things.

Simplicity brings a whole new meaning to life. It is laced with hope. It brings the perfect balance of the masculine and the feminine. It holds a deep satisfaction of completion and contentment within one's self. Living simply takes away the drudgery and the constant challenges of having to do or be a certain way, to fit in or belong. It is accepting life for how it is and being happy with where we are in it.

If you see and accept the beauty all around, you see yourself a part of it.

We are not controlled by religion or society. We don't have to suffer or give ourselves a hard time just because someone tells us how or who we should be. I always saw God to be love. As a child, I couldn't see and feel the fear of God. In school I remember being told by a nun that I was going to hell and I couldn't help thinking that she was going to get there before me! It's quite funny now when I think back at how I felt inside, about what was being said to me and how I perceived what was going on around me. As an adult I am happy within myself that I now have the courage to step out of the control and fear that had been instilled within me in my early life.

I learnt to connect with my own Source (God) through my own heart. It is a natural and rewarding process for all who dare to be different—to learn to love from a place of courage and to know the truth.

Questions

- How difficult do I make life for myself?
- How can I simplify my life?
- Do I want and need so much to be happy?
- How can I discover who I really am?

Affirmations

- I allow things to be simple and clear
- I enjoy the simple things of life
- I love living a simple life
- I see beauty all around me

Chapter 9

The 7 Steps to Financial and Personal Freedom

In previous chapters we explored the various financial aspects of our lives and how our life experiences and choices can often hinder us. For example, let's look at our genetic inheritance and the patterns and behaviours we learnt from our parents. Why did we allow ourselves to believe what others thought and said about us? What boxes did our families, peers, teachers, religion and society put us in? Have we learnt how and why we allowed this to happen? Were we the good child, the black sheep or the rebel? Perhaps we put a 'glass ceiling' in place because we believed that is all to which we could aspire.

It's time to let the old beliefs go by breaking out of the boxes, smashing the glass ceiling and ridding ourselves of self-imposed limitations. Now is the time to build our self-determination, worthiness, uniqueness and belonging. These positive and powerful actions will enable us to step up into our full potential. This brings us to Step 1 of the Seven Steps of A *Spiritual Budget*:

Step 1—The Power of Responsibility

Being responsible is best described as following through with commitment to any given task to the best of our ability. Examples of being responsible include paying bills, keeping our homes neat and tidy, being an example to our loved ones and being in control of our destiny through the choices we make.

The Power of Responsibility also comes from acknowledging that we create our own reality by our thoughts, our actions and our attitudes and that we are not victims to circumstances or people in our lives. Showing determination in finding solutions to problems, being persistent and walking forward (without looking back) are other ways of being responsible.

The ability to take responsibility is being self-determining and having the will to take control of ourselves and the direction of our lives. When we become strong in self-determination we become unwavering, no matter what challenges come our way. We are able to see the truth, take life in our stride and know that we can turn misfortunes into blessings. It is all about raising the altitude of our attitude.

Step 2—Gratitude, Self-Acceptance and Self-Worth

In Step 2 of A *Spiritual Budget* we embrace the qualities of gratitude, self-acceptance and self-worth and allow ourselves to delve deeply into our past, as we explored in Chapter 3. We can acknowledge that we are much more than merely our genetic inheritance. No matter what our background and what we were told about ourselves, we find we can overcome any obstacle and old belief systems by simply changing our attitude and the way we perceive things. By not letting go, we stay in the same place and we re-live all the same experiences over and over again.

If we hold onto something that may have happened many years before, we can become stuck and the possibility for change is stifled. If there is resentment for our past, our self-esteem may be low and we may not feel worthy enough to let go. We may need to build up our self-worth—having a sense of worthiness is an important key to being successful in our life. When we are worthy we are comfortable in our own skin and we value ourselves.

Being grateful is an important part of the process and I have emphasised this many times throughout this book. Gratitude brings a wealth of abundance in all areas of our life—physically, emotionally, mentally and spiritually. Our lives are so much easier on so many levels when we show gratitude.

By allowing ourselves to be who we are (warts and all) gives us the courage to 'feel' into our life experiences. Then, as we acknowledge how we are feeling and show gratitude for what we have learnt, free of judgment, we can then make the choice to go in a new direction. These actions bring self-acceptance and self-worth.

Step 3—Hope and Adaptability

In Step 3 of *A Spiritual Budget* we embrace the qualities of hope and adaptability. In Chapter 5 we explored grief and the effect it has on us. At some stage in life we all experience grief and loss. During times of grief we can experience financial difficulty and its damaging effects can filter through all aspects of our life. It is well documented that in times of financial difficulty, our physical and mental health suffers. The key is to allow ourselves to *feel* how we feel and accept that all feeling is valid. We can learn from grief.

When we embrace hope, even in our darkest hour, a light of hope flickers in the distance to show us the way. This opens new doors and is the first step of the healing process. We need to have courage to *feel* how we feel and then, taking small steps forward with adaptability, we find we are able to move with the change.

Hope works hand in hand with adaptability and belonging. When we have a strong sense of belonging, we know we belong to ourselves—our true selves. We see the light at the end of the tunnel and we are optimistic. We have strong boundaries and authenticity in our words, thoughts and deeds. We are not controlled or ruled by others or groups and feel very comfortable in our skin. No matter where we are, we hold a strong presence and we are very self-sufficient and self-determining.

Step 4—Courage and Persistence

Step 4 of *A Spiritual Budget* involves the qualities of courage, persistence and self-determination.

In Chapter 6 we looked at resistance and how it can stop us from embracing our potential. We can often feel that tug, that pulling back, that feeling in the gut that we can't do it, that we are not good enough and that it's all too hard. By allowing resistance to rule us we miss out on many opportunities. Often we can feel more comfortable with being a victim to our experiences, making dramas of situations and pulling others around us into our stories. We do this so we can justify how right we are with our choices. This is avoidance and denial of the truth and it keeps us small.

Resistance is a habit we learn in childhood. For example, when a child is given a chore or something they don't want to do, they create ways to avoid it. As adults, how do we still avoid and deny stepping into our potential because of resistance? By facing our fears and taking on challenges we are choosing love, respect and self-valuing and we are walking the path of self-discovery. Determination, belonging and worthiness truly hold us strong in our choices. When we change our attitude and acknowledge the resistance, choosing to move forward with courage and being persistent and never giving up, we invite success into our lives. As I have mentioned many times throughout this book—'keep on walking, don't stop and never look back.'

Step 5—Our Uniqueness

Step 5 of *A Spiritual Budget* is about embracing our uniqueness and learning to speak up for ourselves.

Our uniqueness sets us apart. It is our own flavour, our energy signature, but sadly some of us let situations and people squash this most magnificent part of us. When we don't speak up we compromise ourselves. We compromise our uniqueness. We allow the bullies and the undesirables in our society to go unpunished. Speaking up and standing up for what we feel to be just and fair takes courage. Fear of speaking up is learnt behaviour from our childhood. By being patient with ourselves and practicing every day to speak up when the need arises, our confidence grows and we take forward steps in our life. It is the journey, rather than the destination, that is important and it is how we grow.

We can forget who we truly are and we can 'buy into' what our families, peers, religion and society have told us. It is by owning our uniqueness that truly enables us to 'soar like an eagle'. If we follow others, pretending to be different, we are nothing more than turkeys. What's your choice? To soar like an eagle or pretend to be something or someone you're not? As you can see, it is important to speak up and to know your true self and it is how you will fulfil your destiny.

Step 6—Embracing Kindness and Giving

Step 6 of *A Spiritual Budget* is embracing kindness and giving. In Chapter 8 we learnt what it is to truly give. When we give with clear motive our lives will be changed forever. We will begin to seek out more and more opportunities of ways to give. Giving opens us up to more possibilities, for it is only when we give, that we can truly receive. We live in a society of always wanting more and where nothing is ever enough. When this selfish way of living is present, the gift of giving is lost. When we are on the path of self-discovery we soon learn that our lives become enriched and open to receiving when we give openly from a heart-filled place. We become aware of our motives and why we give, opening up many opportunities in our lives and allowing us to become in flow with the Universe.

In Chapter 8 we explored our motives for giving. Are we giving to please or impress others?

We can become a cheerful giver who gives from the heart without any expectation of return. This act of kindness can only bring joy into our lives and into the lives of others.

In our society we have forgotten what giving truly is because we are not strong in worthiness, belonging and uniqueness. Giving and receiving from the heart with gratitude and appreciation is a daily practice and by putting gratitude into practice on a daily basis, our lives will become enriched.

Step 7—Living Simplistically

Step 7 of *A Spiritual Budget* is learning how to live simplistically. Here we look at our wants and needs and our awareness. Some of us have forgotten how to live simply. Life has become complicated and simplicity is diminished by the unrealistic expectations society has imposed upon us. In some ways we have allowed this to happen. We have been told what we have to believe in, how to dress, what we are allowed to say and how we must fit in to be socially accepted. The rules and regulations of life set by others take us away from the gifts of our own individual expression as Spirit in human form.

When there is turmoil in our life it usually affects our financial circumstances. If we have multiple credit cards as well as a mortgage and indulge in frivolous spending, this can set us up for financial adversity, should the unexpected happen. There is nothing wrong with having life's little luxuries. The problem lies in how we go about accumulating them. Budgeting, setting goals, putting a little away each week are all activities in which the whole family can participate. That sought-after item is much more appreciated when the family works toward a common goal by saving for the item, rather being instantly gratified by 'putting it on the plastic'.

Identifying and focusing on what our wants and needs truly are is the first step towards making our lives less complicated. We live in a throw-away society and being grateful for what we already have makes us appreciate all the wonders that are already happening in our lives, rather than looking away and wanting more and more to fill the emptiness within. Being worthy and working with our uniqueness and creativity in learning how we can live a much more fulfilled and simple life is greatly rewarding.

By following these simple steps you will be guided and empowered to move forward into claiming your very own wondrous potential for abundance.

Chapter 10

A Spiritual Budget–
How to be Energy Efficient

In Chapter 2 we looked at our financial budget and how we spend the energy we call money. We are now going to see how we spend our energy (our life force) and we will soon see how A Spiritual Budget and a Financial Budget work together.

If our energy is scattered all over the place and we are giving it away, we can quickly become depleted. An example could be giving our personal power away or compromising ourselves and then becoming resentful, which serves no purpose other than to block the flow of abundance.

There is no difference between a spiritual and financial budget within the flow of abundance—they are two sides of the one coin.

Now let's learn about A *Spiritual Budget*. What is it and how can it work for you?

A Spiritual Budget:

- Is a guide that tells you whether you are heading in the right direction. It teaches you how to live a life empowered by actualising your dreams. It reinforces that you are the captain of your ship, the one at the wheel and making the right choices.
- Gives you control of your own life.

- Makes you aware of how you are using your energy and the effect it is having on you and your environment, giving you a deeper understanding of how your thoughts and energy create your reality.
- Allows you to meet your family, professional, social and spiritual goals as you take responsibility for your choices.
- Gives you extra energy to devote to the things that matter to you as your priorities become clear.
- Prepares you for meeting the challenges of life with greater focus and grace.
- Is a tool for communicating more effectively and authentically from the heart.
- Is a tool of self-discovery, bringing people together so they can combine their energy and work in unison to achieve common goals together.

- Provides you with a way to assess how you are spending your energy and shows you how and where you are wasting it on things that don't support you. It also shows you how giving too much energy to others will only leave you feeling disheartened, exhausted and drained.
- Can help keep you out of spiritual debt by preventing you from creating negative karma and making you more aware of your choices and consequences.
- Assists you to rest easy knowing you are heading in the right direction to achieving your purpose and prosperity.
- Gives you tools and the know-how to be energy efficient.
- Assists you to experience by allowing you to acknowledge what you are feeling in order for you to be able to heal and move forward as a human being, rather than a human doing.

Daily practices to add to your Spiritual Budget Tool Box

Work on your spiritual budget daily.

Keep your energy system squeaky clean—just as you brush your teeth, shower and put on clean clothes, it is equally important to keep your energy system clean.

We don't realise how much of others' thoughts and feelings we carry around with us.

Many of us will have heard about alchemy—raising the frequency of base metal to gold. Our energy system is the same. The lower frequency (the base metal) is fear. The higher frequency (gold) is love. So with our every thought, feeling and action we make a choice and create a frequency between the lower vibration of fear and the higher vibration of love. Clearing our energy system every day gives us the opportunity to know ourselves without others influencing us.

Can any of you identify with going to visit a friend who every week tells you the same story over a cup of tea and then you go home feeling exhausted and they feel great? What is happening here is that you are allowing them to off-load their feelings and negative energy onto you. When we feel sorry for someone we create an energy connection, which then allows him or her access to our energy system. Just as we would not allow a neighbour to empty their rubbish bin in our lounge room, we can choose to maintain appropriate boundaries in our energy system. We can choose to not take on the energy of other peoples' stories.

For protection against those who try to invade your energy system, imagine yourself in a golden bubble of light and mentally repeat to yourself "I return all energy, which is not of me and not of love, back to its original source". If you say this for five minutes you will feel a new sense of lightness and freedom.

The Violet Flame greatly enhances clearing negative energies that you may have picked up from others or your environment and also transforms any negative self-talk or self-criticism. When we work with the Violet Flame we are raising fear-based energies into a higher frequency of love. The simplest way to use the Violet Flame is when you shower in the mornings—visualise yourself surrounded by a beautiful Violet Flame that flows around and through all levels of your being as you connect deeply with the planet. As you are doing this, you consciously release any negative energy you may have taken on or created within yourself and you replace them with love.

This simple process can be run any time during the day when you feel that your energy system needs clearing. *Enjoy!*

Appropriate Boundaries—Self Esteem

When we don't maintain appropriate boundaries we give our power away to others by allowing them to override our choices and our 'knowing'. Have you ever had the experience when someone was up close and personal to you, standing so close that you wanted to take a step back? What is happening is that they are not only crowding your physical space, their energy can also be trying to influence or overpower you. For example, when you walk into a room feeling bubbly and open, then in a short space of time you find yourself suddenly feeling very different. What could have happened is that others in the room may not have been feeling so positive and happy and you therefore take on that energy.

Always be aware and have discernment of what is going on in your environment. It is not about how you are feeling. It is about being aware of others and their energy and then making a conscious choice of what energy you chose to allow in your system.

A wonderful way to keep moving forward into abundance is to write in your gratitude journal those things or people for which you are grateful. Do this each and every day.

Continue with your daily journal acknowledging experiences in the steps you have taken forward.

Each day take a moment to review your checklist for abundance to acknowledge your progress on your journey of self-discovery. If you would like to download and print out a more in-depth Spiritual Budget spread sheet, please go to the free resource:

http://aspiritualbudget.com/
aspiritualbudget/index.php/resources

A *Spiritual Budget* Daily Checklist:

- ☐ Keep your energy system squeaky clean
- ☐ The Violet Flame
- ☐ Self-Acceptance
- ☐ Boundaries
- ☐ Taking Responsibility
- ☐ Speaking Up
- ☐ Giving and Receiving
- ☐ Kindness
- ☐ Simplicity
- ☐ Acknowledgement
- ☐ Self Determination
- ☐ Moving forward
- ☐ Achieving Goals

Wishing you all success with your new 'knowing'.

If you would like to take this further, there are free courses on the Cosmosis Mentoring

Centre website to assist you to expand your understanding and support your unique journey.

The Cosmosis™ Mentoring Centre

Here at the Cosmosis™ Mentoring Centre we work as mentors and educators within a wide range of fields of endeavor to facilitate both inner peace as well as personal and professional success, with special emphasis on self-mastery, philosophy, alchemy, metaphysics and ethics. Cosmosis™ is an internal process for personal growth that enables you to change how you respond to the world. This personal growth process changes your personal reactions and feelings about the people and situations in your life and instead of simply reacting to life, empowers you to consciously choose how you respond. It transforms your old programming and fear-based belief systems. The process has nothing to do with anyone or anything else. It's simply self-meeting self, time and time again, until you get the message that everything in your environment is a reflection of you and that your life is your creation.

As you change your personal response to the people and situations you have attracted to yourself, your journey through life improves. It is very easy to measure your change, because the people and situations pressing your buttons will suddenly appear to be acting differently and your buttons won't get pressed in the same way. This is because the relationship dynamics in your life will have been transformed.

Some of the free courses available at www.mysteryschool.org.au include:

- Abundance and Gratitude—Level 1
- Initial Pitfalls on the Path
- Self-Esteem and The Four Pillars—Level 1
- Energetic Hygiene—Level 1

Each Sunday evening (Australian time) we facilitate a free Cosmosis™ Global Teleconference.

This is the entry level of the Cosmosis™ Personal Spiritual Alchemy Process and we offer it to you for free. Our free class is open to the general public as an introduction to Cosmosis™ Personal Alchemy beginning with the Basic Cosmosis™ Elemental Initiations. This course covers planetary healing, utilising compassion with the Violet Flame and works with self-esteem and ideals. Join in and learn about all things alchemical and metaphysical. www.mysteryschool.org.au

Please feel free to explore the Website!

Welcome Home!

Conclusion

Looking at attitudes towards money—earning it, spending it and giving it away—can offer surprising insights into our lives, our values and the essence of prosperity. *A Spiritual Budget* is a training program within a book and assists you to go deeper into your life in an open and non-judgmental way. It assists you to heal and move beyond the past and guides you to see where you can make changes. It also teaches you how to let go and live a much fuller life, free of self-imposed limitations and the controls of society and the systems that govern us.

A Spiritual Budget is my journey—my story—and how I have experienced my own life and, through my work, what I have learnt from both students and clients. Every single one of us has their own experience, their own stories, that need to be acknowledged and from which valuable lessons are learnt. This is how we grow, love and progress along our own chosen path.

Our material abundance is essentially a reflection of our inner state of abundance. The level to which we feel abundant is typically in place by the age of four and will continue to shape the life we lead unless we take fundamental steps to positively alter that course. Many believe that once we are financially secure we will feel happy and secure within our own selves, but in reality, life works in reverse. As we choose to embrace the limitless depths of security that are truly available within us, our lives begin to reflect the inner shift.

Thank you for reading this book. I truly hope it has helped you move through challenging times and has inspired hope in your heart to make each day a new beginning. Please keep working with the exercises, as they will continue to support you to ever-greater success.

I would greatly appreciate feedback on how this book has inspired and assisted you in making lasting changes and how it has helped you to move ever forward. Email: deb@ aspiritualbudget.com

For tips and resources to assist you with everyday life, please visit *A Spiritual Budget* website: www.aspiritualbudget.com.

Testimonials

"Through working with Debbie, I was able to address the real personal issues underlying my lack of abundance. I now have a quality of life

I could once have only have dreamt of. Thank you Debbie!"

Rupert Guenther, concert violinist & teacher

I love working with Debbie. Her down to earth, non-judgmental approach has helped me to uncover and clear some blocks and blind spots I had around money and abundance, which were holding me back. She has helped me to become accountable for my finances and make changes that are creating more abundance in my life. I have gained a whole lot more self-acceptance and very grateful for her work.

Kim Minos
Naturopath, Herbalist.
ND, Grad Dip WHM, BHSc.

Testimonials from my Workshops

I recently attended Debbie's Spiritual Budget Workshop and left filled with hope and transformation. Debbie has put together a user-friendly, helpful, soul-searching set of tools and framework to get to the very heart of issues affecting our ability to attract and sustain financial abundance in our lives.

I've never had a problem with the business side of things, but earning and attracting money for myself with no limitation has always been a challenge for me. I now understand why, and have helpful steps to heal and to make changes in myself.

I have also learnt about my energy and how to use it. There is enormous heart energy in Debbie's work and these tools are a must for anyone on a spiritual journey who chooses to embrace the potential for love and abundance and accept the truth of what they need to change to make that happen. It's incredibly practical and insightful, yet so pure and wise.

Thank you so much, Deb. I've been working with the steps ever since I left the workshop and I can feel that shifts have begun to happen. Lots of love and heartfelt gratitude for the gifts given.

Lisa Danza Evolve Coaching
and Development

I would like to thank you for a wonderfully presented workshop on *A Spiritual Budget*. It was so well researched, planned and presented with such an open heart that it made for a beautiful day. The gifts I received from the *7 Steps to Financial Freedom* workshop were the motivation to stop procrastinating around my responsibilities, how to take care of my money and to be conscious of where I fritter money away daily. I was inspired to think bigger and was motivated to do a skills audit to focus my energies, identifying all my skills and talents to shift my life and contribution to the community to another level. I am loving paying my bills and doing my tax return today and am so grateful for the privilege of hearing how you have grounded spiritual awareness in practical knowledge, authenticity and personal responsibility. You are a breath of fresh air in the new age movement, Deb. Thank you.

Love from Lorna Bick,
Grief Counsellor

I really enjoyed Deb's workshop. It was well designed, professional and impactful. Deb has a rare gift of being able to keep it simple, to untangle all the ways we complicate life and bring it back to simplicity in a down to earth and grounded way, making it easy for anyone to take the seven steps she shares so lovingly on board and bring abundance in all areas. Thanks Deb!

Big love,

Jenny

CPSIA information can be obtained at www.ICGtesting.com
Printed in the USA
LVOW13s1153180913

352887LV00001B/1/P